PRAISE FOR *L*

"*Love & Metaxa* is a collection of feelings violently thrown against the page. Strigas's work is intense and honest. This collection is a mirror that reminds us of ourselves: a little dirty, a bit sad, stained with coffee, questioning everything, remembering the things that turned into scars, craving booze, ignoring the way the heart aches. These poems are the equivalent of making out with a stranger in a parking lot as wild horses stampede down the street and you feel the weight of the ghosts of old lovers hanging from your lips. Ah, but there is fun and lust, locked rooms and books, the beach and the fact that death is not here yet. Forget reading these poems; feel them. They will probably kiss you in return."

—Gabino Iglesias, author of *Coyote Songs*

"*What does logic have to do with phantoms?* Christina Strigas's *Love & Metaxa* is a magical dive into questioning where we wonder if *Perhaps you are a photographer/ Documenting souls* in a world where *Death sends letters with your name.* Daughter of an immigrant, storyteller, authentically herself, and always open, Strigas writes, *Time has always been a liar*; these poems demonstrate that by effortlessly moving between past and present. Dark and sensual, unafraid, these poems command, *Stop looking for ghosts/under your messy bed. Love & Metaxa* is built around the complexities of humans and makes no apology for our messiness, in fact, these poems embrace it, shine a light into history, turn *headlights into hindsight."*

—Kelli Russell Agodon, author of
Dialogues with Rising Tides

"Strigas's poems are absolutely magnetic. I devoured *Love & Metaxa*, and her words kept coming back to me for days after. The pieces are a hypnotizing mixture of sexy, whimsical, witty, real, and haunting. Savor each one of her poems – they tell an intoxicating story."

—Ginny Hogan, author of
Toxic Femininity in the Workplace

"It's official, I am a devoted aficionado of Christina Strigas's stunning poetry. Having already savored the beautiful addictive collection *Love & Vodka*, I can attest *Love & Metaxa* goes deeper and resonates the kind of lyrical urges only Strigas can craft on the page. Her verses are more than just erotic poetry, Strigas's poems evoke the love, longing, marriage, fantasy, desire, and eloquence of everyday passion that lives between her stanzas and reflect our own carnal cravings of the page. One does not sip Christina's words, no, I urge you to devour *Love & Metaxa*. Strigas's poetry goes through the heart, past the mind by reigniting the body of everyone you loved or ever privately longed to behold."

—Adrian Ernesto Cepeda, author of
Between the Spine

"Christina Strigas is fearless. *Love & Metaxa* gracefully weaves love, trauma, romance, and brutality in an unapologetic poetic force. This book, both tender and fierce, lays everything bare, sacrifices nothing, and demands everything from language through intimate portraits of human chaos. Strigas asks of these experiences not only the why, but the how: intricate maps of longing, death, sex, and the place of the body. Each poem shucks meaning from the root of the world and considers it holy, a gift for the soul. You will want more when the last page turns."

—Joshua Chris Bouchard, author of
Let This Be the End of Me

"Tough-talking, tender, and devastating in its unwavering no-bullshit self-examinations, *Love and Metaxa* is a French kiss in a car crash, a lace-bra wearing rebel with a cause, a fearless street-smart older sister of a book. To be read and read again when you need comfort, a wake-up slap, or both."

—Amber Ridenour Walker, poet

"Christina Strigas's *Love & Metaxa* is a book for dark nights and lit city streets. Evoking the frankness of Ariana Reines—a true muse of post-Bukowski women poets—Strigas writes compelling of poets in the age of internet "high on imagery... looking out the windows anxious / about this and that." A collection that wanders as much as it desires and pursues, *Love & Metaxa* is heart-catchingly bare with itself and its reader, often stripping a poem down to its most vulnerable lines as one strips a bed: "I threw Shakespeare at you...but all you cared about was the white shape of my ass in the air."

—Hannah VanderHart, author of
What Pecan Light

"In *Love & Metaxa*, Strigas confesses the intimate minutes of a flammable girl growing up in a Greek family, and her life beyond in Montreal. It's a nostalgic, heady blend of logic and magic, love and eros, the living and the dead, all poured out for us in emotive "gold shots." It's the story of painful almosts where you're both fine and not fine at all. Sensual memories flicker for the reader like film vignettes glowing in the amber wash of Metaxa. Honeysuckle and kitchen spices bouquet these poems, but also the slow burn of something darker. Carnal secrets pound into cutting boards and hotel beds. Above all, the poet sings about the binding and unbinding of relationships – the ones that are quick and the ones that haunt us. *Love & Metaxa* shares a poignant desire to "get to the bottom of love."

—Leah Callen, poet

"The only words that should be used to describe Christina Strigas's poetry – in this volume or any of her others – are Christina's words themselves. Some readers will find the emotional (and sexual) honesty in *Love & Metaxa* simply too overwhelming, too raw. But surely, even they will recognise and respect the palpable longing, tender confession and un-flinching confrontation of truths exposed by these poems. You want poetry to soothe and comfort? Read another poet."

—Mark Antony Owen, author of *Subruria*

"Not only a love letter to the titular Greek spirit, but a powerful testimony on moving beyond what we once were. In *Love & Metaxa*, Strigas uses the endless powers or language to first remind you of how dark life can be, then assure you that somehow everything may just work out for the best."

—Stuart Buck, Poet, author of *Blue the Green Sky*

"Christina Strigas's poems are raw, sultry, and self-reflective. *Love & Metaxa* takes you into a Greek lyrical festival and ignites you with Metaxa and Ouzo. This book is a collection of dark and titillating poems that explore the essence of what it means to be a woman and poet in this day and age."

—Nancy Levine, author of *The Tao of Pug*

"In a stripped-down yet profound verse, the speaker in *Love & Metaxa* shows us the lust and magic of her Greek-Canadian life, but there is also lingering, painful familial memory. Similarly, the poet highlights the fast-paced world of poetry and its relationship to internet culture, and does not overlook how art currently serves as a commodity and a privilege. In this always urgent, sometimes subtle collection, Strigas wants us to see and feel the heart and soul of things, and, at the end of the day, chase it down with a crisp glass of Metaxa, smooth and refined."

—Jose Hernandez Diaz, author of *The Fire Eater*

"Christina Strigas's *Love and Metaxa* is a collection of poems shot through with lyric intensity and grace. The speaker's voice here is singular and unflinching, often exploring—from a decidedly feminist perspective—deep rooted traumas, those psychic cages the culture uses to trap and diminish us. It's a powerful book, one in which many readers will see their own lives."

—Erin Belieu, author of *Come-Hither Honeycomb*

"*Love & Metaxa* is an exploration into the depth of wanting, even if it's bad for you. Strigas is a natural storyteller, her poems revealing the various characters and emotional environments of her life. This collection touches on the pains of loving and wanting as a woman in a world where women are encouraged to form around male rage and emotional confusion. A beautiful book of poetry that I treasure."

—Erin Taylor, author of *Bimboland*

"I will turn your chaos to glitter." – Through her poetry, Christina Strigas paints stories of human relationships, of love and loss, intrinsically linked."

—Isabelle Kenyon, author of *Growing Pains*

"Christina Strigas's *Love & Metaxa* has a language that reverberates within it: a language of longing, of intimacy, and of place. There is an incredible music to it. Each poem moves to its own rhythms, but the momentum grows and grows. We do not stop moving. Strigas moves us through time, beyond death. These poems hold the dark and the light in one place and help reveal what they can teach us. There is no deeper magic."

—Catherine Garbinsky, author of
All Spells Are Strong Here

"Christina Strigas's *Love & Metaxa* is a collection you will want to read and savor multiple times. Her poems are hauntingly beautiful, with elements of nostalgia, and erotica. In her poem *White Cell Counts* she seduces the reader by appealing to our senses, with stanzas like "From your smile, /Our skin turns wet now/Honeysuckle entangles our bodies." Her imagery is powerful, and there are times throughout the collection one can't help but feel they are on the precipice of danger. *Love & Metaxa* is thoroughly enchanting."

—Marisa Silva-Dunbar, author of *Becky*

"In *Love and Metaxa*, Christina Strigas looks back on her life and teaches herself and her readers hard truths. Self-esteem is a "secret piranha," death "ticks its clock each morning," and "*Everything you have ever written or worn / Shines brighter when you are dead.*" Yet these harsh truths are softened by the beauty around us and between us, "Who needs to know the latitude of heaven / when the city lights / shine down upon our winter skin?" This collection is the perfect balance of pain and beauty, a treasure on every page."

—Shaindel Beers, author of *Secure Your Own Mask*, finalist for the Oregon Book Award

LOVE &

METAXA

BOOKS BY CHRISTINA STRIGAS

POETRY
Your Ink on My Soul
In My Own Flood
Love & Vodka

NOVELS
The Wanting
Crush: A Paranormal Romance Novel
Althia's Awakening
Althia's Calling
Althia's Journey

SELF-HELP
A Book of Chrissyisms

LOVE &
METAXA

poems by
CHRISTINA STRIGAS

For permission requests, email the author:
chrissystriga@gmail.com
with the body:
"Attention: Permission Coordinator"

Editor: Alexandra Meehan

ISBN: 978-1-7331037-9-4

CANADA CATALOGUING IN PUBLICATION DATA
Strigas, Christina, 1968-, author
Love & Metaxa / poetry by Christina Strigas

POEMS PREVIOUSLY PUBLISHED IN LITERARY REVIEWS

Thank you to the editors of the following journals and magazines where some of these poems were first featured, at times, in earlier versions.

"Decades of Art" and "No Vacancy" featured by *Neon Mariposa Magazine*, January, 2019.

"No Vacancy" was nominated for Best of the Net 2019 by *Neon Mariposa Magazine.*

"Fasting" featured by *Pink Plastic House*, May 23, 2019.

"Monster" and "Conversations with the Dead" featured by *Rhythm & Bones,* Issue 2 of Dark Marrow, March 2019.

"Corinth" featured by *Thimble Lit Magazine,* Spring Issue No. 4, March 2019.

"The Apologies" featured by *Chantarelle's Notebook*, April 23, 2019.

"Patera I" featured by *The Temz Review*: Issue 6, January 2019.

"Oh, Canada" and "Patera II" featured by *Montreal Writes,* February issue, 2019.

"Love & Metaxa" featured by *Rhythm & Bones Lit,* Issue 3: Dark Marrow, July 2019.

"Amuse Me," "Appointment," and "Yiayia Maria" featured by *BlazeVox19* Fall 2019, November 12, 2019.

"Nature is Calling" featured by *Visitant,* January 28, 2020.

"Personify Me" featured by *Visitant*, Feb. 19, 2020.

"Let the Clouds Speak," "Going Under," "Tumble," and "Cape Cod" featured by *Neon Mariposa Magazine*, Issue 4: March 2, 2020.

"Les Enfants Terribles," "Small Miracles," "On Being Starstruck," "On Stardom," "Magic," "The Day After," "Every Woman," "Rumi Lovers," "Her Side," and "Blue-Aged Love" featured by *Feminine Collective.*

You have to die a few times before you can really live.

—CHARLES BUKOWSKI

I dedicate this book to the publishing houses that
accepted this manuscript
rejected it, accepted it, rejected it
and finally accepted it
then rejected it.

Three versions, three acceptances, three rejections.

I did it on my own again because that is what
the universe wanted,
you cannot resist the force of
creativity or its energy.

You must embrace the rejections
and make them yours.

———————————————————

In truth, I dedicate this book to my dog Spunky
who loves and protects me like an angel.

CONTENTS

FOREWORD

Christina and I met through the internet in shared writing groups. I suspect it was cosmic attraction because we had so many things in common: we share similar politics, we are both Mediterranean Virgos, we enjoy the same rock music and poets, and we are both engrossed in the macabre. We instantly clicked, and soon after, we were challenging one another through offbeat writing prompts. We talked every day—whether chatting about cooking or painting, it always had something to do with being creative. Our daily conversations were intimate, uplifting, funny, depressing, dark. We became the best of friends.

Write something so intimate, so vulnerable,
that it feels embarrassing—it feels too much.
Then make it stronger.

I remember Christina's surprise when she received the edited version of *Love & Metaxa*. She was distraught—it had been whittled into internet-pop micropoetry, entirely unlike her original manuscript. Since we had already developed a writing relationship, Christina hired me as her second pair of eyes. I suggested adding newer pieces, so we hunted through hundreds of unlabeled documents, meticulously selecting poems we thought melded well. We added, subtracted, and went from there; it became a completely new project. And even though we were busy with all of this, we still set time aside for our poetry prompts.

Working on this was a learning experience. I did not know what Metaxa was—none of the liquor stores here carried it, nor did I know her French and Greek colloquialisms. I had never heard of mythomania, and while I studied Ancient Greek in college and knew most of the famous mythologies, I was not familiar with the lesser-known stories. I spent hours scouring the web for the romantic, heart-wrenching ballads that she referenced. I submerged myself into histories that I had long forgotten. I was swimming in Greek culture—it is sensual, dramatic, and splendidly intense. And death is a film noir.

We focused on translating *Love & Metaxa* into what she had wanted it to be: a testament to her Greek culture, her sense of soul and being—Christina, a Greek-Canadian feminist, a mother and a wife, and the daughter of old-world Greek immigrants. Much like a diary, *Love & Metaxa* is a record of Christina's life and ever-changing perceptions, her landscapes and mental states—a journey that is as magical as it is tragic. These poems explore Christina's suffering and love, the rituals of life and death, and the "brilliance of the darkness." This is her love letter to poets and also her revenge; her rejection letter and acceptance speech.

Three different literary presses picked up *Love & Metaxa*, though it was never officially published. Due to the growing pandemic, the first press halted publications. The second press was publicly canceled, and the third press simply collapsed. The book floated between hands for years, and with each parting, the poems changed. After three cancellations, we were right back where we started. By this point, we reverted to the first revised manuscript and edited it again. We bounced back and forth, typing between sips of wine in the night, a poem between each story of the day. After what felt like an actual odyssey, the book finally found its forever home — and now you are holding it. You are holding cosmic attraction.

This collection is not to be served on the rocks and diluted, rather poured neat; a slow and sensuous burn to experience in the dark. It is a voyage beyond our tech-obsessed world back to the wild, ancient beaches of Greece. *Love & Metaxa* is about destiny, chance, and prediction, about how the universe twists all our arms. This book is her heart in a glass, a dive into the art of drowning.

— Alexandra Meehan

LOVE & METAXA

I tasted you at sixteen
when my cousin died of cancer,
everyone had hollow eyes
like the depth of
empty jars.

Months, years. Uncle G
was the one who didn't speak.
He swallowed too much death
in his ancient bloodline
before the age of twenty-three,
silent death. I tried you —

Funeral one, you said *hello*
from the bottom
of a tiny shot glass,
while film reeled at your wake.

Dead first cousin,
first of first's in the coffin,
yellow copper skin
tubes and ICU rooms
I cannot drink away —
Metaxa

I embraced you while dancing Greek
knees dirty on the ground

wild hands in the air
mouth around your home,
clapping beats
in the air—

You warmed me up
made all the pain dissipate;
seconds—minutes—heat
waves took deep rooted hurt away.

go go go
put your lips on me, girl

I lifted you
brown neck exposed,
silent paths to
your taste
flooding down, spinning barefoot
your entrance,
a secret winter lover.

One lucid party after another,
a memorial
one wedding, the Zorba dance,
one more mechanical shot—
Forty more days of customary darkness.

Never cheers at a Greek funeral,
there are crystal rules.
Knowing when to appear

your ancient ghosts
kissing dried cheeks,
charming nights as lovers do.

An imaginary friend,
comforting me and
making me sick.
I vomited you up, and backed out away—
until I dreamt of it more
to bring back our dead
in one more shot.

go go go...

THE DAY AFTER

You've gone.
Blocked the cool rain
From touching my skin,
It senses your dragging kiss.

In this caffeine rush,
You came and went
Not reading the menu,
My overpopulated mind.
All these nonsensical words
Lined up in disarray,

For you.
Written on lined paper
With damned hopelessness
For you,
With nothing but harlequin snakes.

People here have empty ten a.m. eyes,
Five p.m. smells
Seven p.m. struts.
Do you ever feel
As if you are the only one
Who can see it?

Perhaps you are a photographer
Documenting souls
Lining them on clotheslines,
Linen pants, jeans
Old rock t-shirts,
Spotless sheets, bright blankets
Painting vacant faces,
Perhaps you are an artist.

Maybe you create music
On paper, in your heart
In your cluttered garage,
Maybe you're like me
Writing poems,
Unswept prose
Short stories about Greece
Playful books,
Sullied spots of words

On your phone
Tablet,
In your weary notes
On the mirror
A computer,
Inside the walls.

Perhaps you think
You're the best out there,
Your own personal
Best bullshit.

I shattered those dreams long ago
To reawaken,

To start all over.

GARAGE LOVE

I was not even mad
when I wrote you my first love letter in winter.
For once
I was in love with the idea of love,
the thrill of its zestful ambiguity.

I knew that anything simple
would bore me
like taking out the trash,
labored dinners,
comfort is full of dullness.
It was folded
unfolded

and only three messy written pages.

It was more of an angry poem
that turned into a love letter,
a gloom of dissatisfaction
that turned into self-indulgence.
Act now —

I found it tucked, shunned from your heart
in your garage, next to the tool box
you had forgotten my pain.
I gulped dry air

down my own throat.
Bam. There it was

unhappiness and fruitless chores,
my heavy-footed heart
murmured incoherent quibble.
I reread it and knew only wrath
changes with time
too many love letters turned,
headlights into hindsight:
words prosy, pointless, coddling,
seducing.
Giving up. Bam. There it is,
Another shot—

A commonplace apology letter,
with old moth holes
ratty
pungent
from that winter drunk

who beat me again.

MAGIC

I was a child once
with flaming sunshine in my eyes
and pure dirt on my bare feet,
running past sprinklers
half-naked
half-hearted
half-dressed
bare-breasted,

then magic crept in,
inside
to cure loneliness,
to eat heartache.

I gave so much of myself to coming darkness,
but sunshine kept peeking in on me
checking in on me,
up on me
quietly, came climbing closely
a white shadow.

Tripping words stung with beauty
bird songs carried me,
caged
in the nest of your arms,
I was hanging on by tied bedsheets

bloodstained,
frilled strings of lost childhood.

I've grown
matured into a flawed woman
with jasmine oil on her wrists
and coffee stains on her jeans.
Send me framed words on immaculate paper
more cryptic messages,
sublime photos
unsent cards
loose leaves of my lost stumbles,
I'm waiting here with abandonment.

UNCLE

Card game going on upstairs
Warm fire and blanket downstairs,
My fourteen-year-old body,
Tight Sergio Valenti jeans
Immature curves, baby face
Asleep on the couch.
Vulnerable as can be,
In sleep
Is how dangerous the game gets.

Rough hands
Rub my legs in an unfamiliar way,
No one with me, in the basement
Except for Uncle,
Who asked me if I was cold
With a look in his eyes screaming
Run—

Into the khaki green kitchen
Full of 80s smoke
Card games
Shouts about crazy-eight hands,
A steel chair wrapped tight,
Clanking
Water running
Greek music, blaring

Squeezing my hands over my mouth,
Mother: *You okay?*
Nothing.
Dying inside
Wondering if Uncle
Was planning to rape me,
Drunk

Maybe only molest me,
No voice answers back.

I stayed there all night
Rocking
Ashamed,
Alert and awake
Observing them play cards,
At the table their gold hands flailing
While my breath trickled off...

Vivacious Greek faces
Suspect of nothing.
My obscure guilt eating
My adolescent voice quiet

For countless
Long nights,
Are you sick, honey?
You look pale.

Overcast years.

UNCLE II

At his funeral,
I damned him
I doomed him
I did not forgive,
Biting my lip, glad he was dead.

He gave me this dark secret,
This poison.
I never told, but kept
His hangover
Blanket blank stare.
Brooding silence,
Internal guilt

It made me vomit.
Cursed to ask *why me?*
Made me distrust men.
I detest myself for falling asleep
To be around him for thirty years,

Events
Marriages
Funerals
Parties

Protecting him from father's wrath,
Wanting

For father to pass him,
Come over,
So that he would tell him
That hell was the other door.

Wishing I had told father
I was almost raped,
But maybe it isn't a big deal,
Because nothing happened.
It only almost happened.

LET THE CLOUDS SPEAK

Love can be so cruel to eight-year-old girls
who remember every cut their parents sliced.
Funeral cake with bloody confetti
unintentional, conditional
paraphrased love.
To be balanced on one foot,

until we all fall over.
In forty years,
so much can affect you.

The moon is full tonight.
Let the clouds speak why they feel hidden
under such a magnificent moon,
what can they say to each other
in a language of lovers
only we comprehend?

Death sends letters with your name,
you could not imagine
how your syllables inhabit my soul.

You can never read my poems with a
magnifying glass or telescope.
Your name is my password,
hidden letters of Earth,
I was eight and now I'm not.
Parents make you almost human.

WHITE CELL COUNTS

There is poetry on your bare feet,
Apocalyptic imagery that begs
Kisses words
Aches to merge with mine.

Sing to me the meaning of your poem,
I will turn your chaos to glitter.
Our skin turns wet now
Honeysuckle entangles our bodies.
Intoxicated in my words
Against my chest,
You are massaging me
With my own typewriter oil.

Verbal orgasms,
On heritage rocks
Sex on the beach, Caribbean rum and Coke,
Long Island iced tea.
Greasy bars reflecting city lights
Limes, salts.
You cannot see how the snow
Eats up flowers beyond the peeling window.

You and I, we sync
We are drunk
On our world of make-believe.
Please keep whispering to me,

How my artistic ways leave you naked.
Unattended
Watch, as I turn my orgasms
Into poems.

NATURE IS CALLING

Grass of mysterious light
Do you become dry from lack of love?

Nature has this bearing on all of us,
Take out white paper

Draw the red cardinal bird
Singing wet songs for your neighbors.

Purple lilacs left a trace of color
But for once

They were alive with love for you,
You passed by them every day

In a sky filled with desirable dreams
Look at hidden unmasked beauty.

Stop your dirty car,
Examine the dark cypress trees

Their tall timeless magnificent presence
Hovers tracing doubt.

Keep the charcoals close to your heart,
You'll never know when

You'll become a budding artist.
Even at a frightful age,

The horizon will have your name,
Its colors transform a petty mood.

Stop writing your grocery list,
Sit down, breathe flowers

May tulips or June blooms.
Tomatoes and cucumbers

Bay leaves and fresh basil plants
Smell the time of year,

It's waiting for you to look up.
Listen to the sound of the songless bird

Its silence is filled with your thoughts,
Become young again

Be a gardener of the Earth for now,
Let the words settle and take a break.

KANGAROO

Do not take an expedition—
I know what is in your pocket,
your ace is peeking out.
The women are lining up for autographs,
the men are hating

how you tie your designer shoes,
grow your handsome grey beard.
How you know exactly what to say
to women with power,
how to weaken them with lust.

You are the type of evil animal
we see coming
running—
But it's best to face the devil
in the red eye.

A MAN

I want to be a man,
I want to wear a tie.
Combine and match
the way my grandfather
taught me to tie,
I long to have strong
able arms,
lift heavy objects—

Shovel fresh fallen snow,
repair my antique car
build a tool shed
throw women in the air.
I want to easily
impress my woman
with my masculine physique.

Did I believe in my mother?
Have an absentee father?
Foster parents? In insecurities and
in death — Did I believe
that boys don't cry?

I want to know what it feels like
to be hard for her
to enter her—
To have so much passion and desire

for her tiny body
that I could mow the lawn bare chested,
paint the house in my ripped overalls
bring her morning flowers,
taste every dark mole residing on her body.

I want to know how it feels
to breathe in and out
from a man's chest,
to bear these sexual thoughts.
Thrusting all day

I wish to watch sexy porn,
masturbate freely
and not feel
an ounce of guilt.
Have angry sex before dinner is served.

Flirt with pretty girls
have an affair on the side,
break her heart and home,
walk around in my briefs
naked.

I want to pay for my woman's meals,
buy her gifts, run my rough fingers
through her grey hair.
I want to take photographs
of my sexy lover
naked, in black and white

shots
wearing nothing but knee-highs
and black-framed glasses.

What does this feel like?
This natural power
to be a loyal father
a husband
a lover,
a sex machine?
To have and to hold her
then fuck up and lose her?

UGLY IS BEAUTIFUL

As I swallow your venomous words
I shrug them off like lint on my shirt,
all of you

I have a horse in my mouth
when my daughter tells me, innocently
I am weak,
nice.
I hate myself for its passive mix,
quick witted feelings stampede—
hooves trot on top my psyche.

I am beautiful to them
mixed with whirly whiskey—
Him drinking and asking
Did you dream of my fuck?
Come to my lips.
Thank you for not being honest.

We know how truth
bends lies like a paper clip
or removes secrets like a staple,
but your sharp words are still blunt,
with your lessons I've learned this:
I might be drunk on a past life
or sober in the next,
but I'm learning

how all of this
means nothing.

I could be a different woman,
no frills or flower strings,
no orchid scent staining my skin
attracting men
for attention,
my simple pheromones will do.

Set an alarm for daybreak,
examine his freckles
the Mohawk gelled to his balding head.
He said, *You wear cozy jeans*
but what kind of man
only uses cozy?
What was he thinking
when I said
These chandeliers are brilliant.

In a poem you look for peace.
In life, all you find is chaos.

DO NOT DISTURB

Turn my face any way you want,
I like what makes him
want me as a teenager.
Telling me what he desires:
how fast
how slow
how hard
how soft

younger, banging and more fucking.
Sometimes you follow your heart,
destroy your logic.
Down the path toward the elevator
room numbers and do not disturb signs,
I water my soul with imaginative kisses.

I'm fine. I'm not fine at all.
Inexperienced in the ways of his world,
his black hair on mine
his height intimidating me,
making me feel like a child.

But he says *he likes that about me*
that I'm like a child—
Stop with the carnivorous lies!
Even your poems
have rejected me.

I never existed,
omit me.

So many old lovers to choose from:
smart asses
pretty faces,
salt and pepper lies
unmatched truths
lost paper trails—
unproblematic characters
with tidier homes.
It's all in my notebooks
wanting to be analyzed
by strangers.

HIDE & SEEK

Do you ever feel how dead silence
has many meanings in your private dictionary?
The way it gulps down your worries and tames
the animal?
It is as powerful as the glass you cannot refuse,
do not be afraid—
you are not the only addict in this book.
There are more spirits touching the page
than leaving it behind.

Silence can proclaim your need
to never awake again,
the same again and again—
Walking away from your kitchen table
you carry a pack of smokes,
a drink
sealed letters
pens.

Then later enter the first Parisian café shop
that looks authentic, hip and
family-run

you sit down and you write
about the ex-lover you had over and over—
twenty times. Every touch of the ceiling, all the edges
as you jumped on his bed, your hands

rubbing the prickly plaster
you remember

how he left you with his ChapStick
as if it were a gift from the gods,
this slippery taste of him.
And while you might not wear it anymore,
you took it home to hide it.

METAXA

I will give you all my love,
your unwanted trust
I will annihilate.
Hand it over —
your sad disgruntled sex
positions,
I will drink it away
take it down —
hot and intense
bitter addictive
Metaxa,
you're welcome
shaking in the courtroom
I'd never fathomed
living in bars,
it all ends —
how this secret loving
did warp
my fragile psyche,
drinking alone —
Metaxa,
in my own tragic
head and heart,
I own you.

A SIP

Knobby knees
slanted eyes
giraffe legs—
film reels…
commercials
moments
music
our backyard graves,
old Greek songs making
senses discover
what
who
when
stabbing my flaws,
annihilate my body!

Think about it!
Drink something light like
Greek coffee
sink, dive head first—
into a bouzouki,
I'm parched for your attached devotion.

Scream beautifully—
attach words to sunlight
your phrases to moonlight,
then fuck off I've had enough.

Slide off the mosaic mask,
we are there again.
Blue and white 60s tiles
smudged mirror
not yet abandoned,
needing a new look.
Smash it,
reinvent yourself.

TATTERED HAT

Pull the ten-year-old weeds
from their dampened core,
that cute old couple,
they are sweetly working up a sweat.
Unlock the patterns of the garden,
make fresh vegetables out of a smile.

She wears her thirty-year-old grey flowered gloves
he wears his gardening tattered hat,
they're talking in Plants and Vegetables
the way poets talk Volta:

Don't use too much water
you will kill the tomatoes,
wait for the summer rain
before it's seven p.m.
the city gives you a fine.

Plant seeds in May
then water in August,
listen to a tip from the wise —
a basil flowerpot is essential
(fresh herbs are more a part of cooking
than other ingredients are).
Hang your clothes outside,
let the sun and fresh air dry them
as I inhale your familiar scent,

you're prettier
when you talk in Earth and Weeds.

LES ENFANTS TERRIBLES

Grand Prix night, 2017
out for dinner and drinks on Bernard Street
picturesque Outremont humid night in Montreal.
Everyone was out in the city —
Revving their hungry engines,
weather we wait all year for
tired of the winter months.

French and English crowds on open terraces
bottles of red and white wine, cold beer, colorful
Martini drinks,
we stayed near the backstreets
where our names are carved in tree trunks.

It's weirdos like us who inhabit these alleys
meet, greet, *Bonsoir!*
Our decades of walking them up and down
from teenage angst to mid-life crisis
the sign says,
We can only park for twenty-three hours and
59 minutes...pas de stationnement.

The men from Marseilles recounted stories
painting impressionistic pictures —
still portraits, surrealism, landscapes;
stumbling ladies on cobblestone terraces
young hipsters smoking cigars,

we were eating our entrées, chucking at the nightly nonsense
made from the moon shining upon the night.

Their leather faces lined with laughter
how an eighty-four-year-old French man, Prospero, is
looking for a wife:
Hey, is your mom single?
Huh? My mom? Yeah, right.
Another man sitting across bellowing
Arrange tes cheveaux! Prospero smacking his boy,
a rolled-up paper like a hollow pipe
whacking his head
we giggled. Lied our way out of the chattering resto,
men out of control with their theatrics,
got St-Viateur bagels warm with spread.

Then Waverly Bar for a last call,
for drinks on another house
on another popular street
in another Montreal alley,
Bonne nuit.

PHONE CALLS

I tucked her words under my blouse,
bra, lace panties.
I sealed them with monograms
hung them outside for fresh air,
slept with their warmth.

My mother calls me
and I stop everything.
Pick up the phone—
desperate to hear her familiar voice,
I worry one day
this addictive phone will stop ringing,
Where are you?
How did you sleep?
What is that sound?
What are you cooking?
The kitchen window winks,
stop waiting for time to apologize.

It's pointless to wait for a full moon
when you know it long passed.
It's hard to live with death—
and yet it ticks its clock each morning,
and then the phone rings.
I answer preparing to relate
the ingredients of the day,
to tell her what's been cooking.

I TELL MYSELF

It's always easy to write it
frame it,
thrift shop photos
Facebook fame
sell it
create a bookmark
trust no one—
sign an email with a username
electronically
an angel, the stranger behind the screen
a devil.

Auction your book to the highest bidder.
Give it away, give it away, giveaway—
you're the wanted poet,
plastered to your phone
for soulful ransom
make putty out of
words,
sellout—
pinch and punch out
your Bitcoins for art.

RINSING

How do you remove stains
when you cannot see them?
The load is fat and full,
my palms are empty —
scrub me raw
with words,
repeat:
strip
bleach
dry
fold

Love me up and down with your need,
lather me with water of the universe
to rinse me,
dry off my desire.
Use toxic detergents,
my skin has become infected.
Put me in your side drawer.

You've rubbed your lover's stain
into my sheets again,
and step-by-step you know
what will come next,
then repeat.

MONSTER

Stop looking for ghosts
under your messy bed,
it's full of secretive dust balls.
Stop looking out the closed window,
cease worrying about invasions

robberies
wars
refugees,
your mind is a prison cell

smothering your screen,
current events, news anchors
babbling like dummy heads,
pop stars
the bombardment of
layered fake news
like lemon sponge cake,
it's enough now.

Remember how the familiar grass
felt under young bare feet
at three-years-old?
When your Mommy held the hose
and wet your tiny feet?
Your senses were alive,

her love unconditional
for the first and only

close your eyes now.
Think of her younger eyes
her lullaby
of dearly hate,
reach out for a hand —
It matters not.

Even as your monster
she drank your tears for morning coffee,
swallowed your spirit for breakfast
lying pretty hope
on the dirty kitchen table.
Ask her,
aren't we all monsters?

Monsters are the loneliest creatures,
we're not all under your bed
or in your head,
we're all looking at you
straight in the empty eye,
in your mirror
in your head
lift the covers or just stop checking,

you still love her.
Never forget your tiny feet,

one enemy is enough,
go ahead—
call her to tell her
you think about her every day,
then go back to hating her.

SUBURBIA RENOWNED

He missed his flight,
Alone in a terminal chair
Contemplating the woman
Who loved him most.

She was distracted
Washing the bath,
Bleaching
Forgetting the dry cleaners,
Errands
Pregnant
Missing blouse buttons
Submerged in receipts,
Her husband watching—

His perfect housewife.
Twenty-years categorizing,
Vacuuming dust
Ash
Broken glass
Shedded hair
Bread crumbs,
Up at dawn to bake.

He was born in a small town in the States
(Canadians were too good to be true),
They were lovers for only a day.

He told her *don't turn around*
It was getting too late,

She never meant to pretend.
Lies came out of her mouth
Like smoke in an engine.

Now she boils dead lobsters for her husband.
Step-by-step she makes
Her secret lobster recipe,
It's Suburbia renowned.

When you're eighty
Irrelevant and Lonely
With shells of regret,
Write a grocery list
And never forget the lobsters.

JUNE CLEAVER

Counter is dirty
Pounding the meat—
Smack!
For nightly dinner

Be a good wife,
Good girl bad girl
Naughty girl
Little girl
Good mother,
Explain the news
Update the bras
Shave the bush,
Smile

Incessantly
I'm admiring philosophers
Free in their spirit
Mine locked away,
Bang!
On the counter,
Sex again
Cooking again
Wishy-washy over the sink,
The chicken's raw with disease.

Make a new chicken
Squeezing egotistical lemons,
Spicing virtue
Pinching the oregano and garlic
Clanking the pots,
Dishes clatter.

This is how I gulp you down,
Thud!
I am left with pounding meat.

THE KISSING LOVERS

She imagined him lifting cars,
saving victims on his coffee break.

He imagined her
having a panic attack at the front door.
She shut it and opened it five times,
counted the locks,
obsessed with odd things
that only mattered to her.

Another flight to Montreal to admire
her stride across a foreign room,
lavish white Egyptian sheets
four lush pillows
an antique desk,
hotel logo on a pen
already in her purse
for a keepsake.
It was a match that no one knew
except them.

Lovers whose lips met for hours
fully clothed in classy hotel rooms.
A Romeo, an innocent Juliet in
middle age
modern times,
dearest darling

stay infatuated with what will never be,
whose life is
uncherished, estranged and secluded
who would kiss with their clothes on at forty—
Who would forsake true love for sex?

He wanted her naked. Lovingly
she wanted to escape without names—
Paris, *rue Champs Elysee*
arriving at *l'Arc de Triomphe*
Gare de Lazare, stops
et *George V café.*

Not stew.
Boil and cook bloody oxtail
in a one-room apartment,
party preparations
aching
to be free like him from morning until flight.

For lovers are created in locked rooms,
not only on paper.

A QUILT FULL OF ADDICTIONS

Your soulmate is kissing someone else up against dirty gym class lockers, in a sleazy hotel room on date night, their sweaty bodies grinding and touching, hands in each other's wild hair with young ecstasy.

Frail love and fear you accept. Nothing is as hidden as you presume. You accept you can never be loved the way you love back, your self-esteem failed—your secret piranha grows. You try to hide it, boiling away the desires consuming, the limbs search for a floor, but legs just dangle in anticipation—

You watch the others smile, observe the movement, misinterpret what they say. Their lips become something you want to taste, one glance and you've concocted a trifold love affair. Promises of unrequited love, the dissolved girl in the Massive Attack song, the boy who cries out *The Thing*—that's you.

You go on like nothing vulgar ever happens—you drag off cheap cigarettes and kiss angsty boys, hiding at parties, drinking peach and peppermint schnapps, taking acid and concocting juvenile poetry, high on floating words and sex scandals, burning holes through pages, journals of how your heart aches of murder.

NOT A LOVE AFFAIR

You feel love to be a phantom. What if that person
never destroyed you? What if that spirit wasn't
deserving? *Love? What is that?* Decades later, when you
run into an old ghost, you will feel frightened—fifteen
with acne again. You'll know. You will feel an ache.
Nothing will have changed but the grey hair on your
heads. You still eat licorice. You both pass each other as
strangers do, you feel close to a lover you may have
never kissed. It makes no sense. It terrifies your logic.
What does logic have to do with phantoms? You intend to
get to the bottom of love. You approach and ask the
ghost to sit down, you smile, and then you say *hello*.

BLUE-AGED LOVE

I search for you
like a lost lover of jazz
I find you in the dim
as you play a deceiver of love,
where love is never free,
prices to pay at every bank vault.

Waiting for musical clouds
to form in all the shapes
we always talked about.
A feeble goodness
shining phosphorescent on the future,
I know we will not meet
for another twenty years,
when death creeps up on us.

I wait for your weeping rays,
dingy in broken wood
the love that kills words
ill-defined and toothless.
Your music
soothes my inky soul.

I asked you to stay awhile,
to admire the closeness
of our mayhem energy.

I still see you now
indistinct from across centuries,

we faded into change.
Into blue pockets filled with music
behind poetry's veil
we sewed our denim love
to golden sun buttons,
glowing coins on rings
in dim bank vaults,
mahogany and friendship
shifted into bank accounts
of locked chances.

INHERITANCE

You inherited a twelveplex
the kind that rents
for one-hundred-twenty minimum per month,
your unheated
cold flat.
Bring your rent upfront
now housing is en vogue—
for *les nouveaux riches*.

Three-and-a-half for eight-hundred max,
you want to see a renovated love?
Each one of your apartments
needs big bucks— big love,

there's a minimum
but you want to squeeze it dry.
A poem about money
is too unromantic,
too legal,
institutional.

Who wants to pay inheritance tax?
Crystallization of inheritance?
That's unromantic,
you do

money
capital gains
trust companies for the kids
funds and property,
prisoner of stocks and
empty bonds.
Investment for this uncertain future.

But if I turn it into a poem
it does sound lovelier
in a moneyless place,
waiting in line at the bank
I may write you a love-money poem,
free to touch wherever, whomever
astonished by how
freedom needs no money
even in a designer jean pocket.

KEEPSAKES

Everyone goes to the beach
to swim and tan,
get golden brown
smolder
burn,
seduce the opposite sex.

Same sex.
I go to the beach
sunscreen, hats and colorful pens.
Stare past the strange ocean
read novels
modern poetry books.

Hide from the sun
collect ivory conch shells,
place them in Ziploc bags.
Gather a new freedom to begin again
like my loathsome self again

tan on volcano sand,
break past unequivocal waves
burst into the summer moment
thunderclap of sky.
Blast forward with ambition
to where the admiring Olympians
only reward hope.

PROMISES

I love with my soul first,
it's instant
you'll abhor it,
its split-second faculty.

I'll show you my paintings
portraits
apathetic mirrors,
bang me on my bedroom floor.

Use vulgar porn words
naughty love
come at me
from all directions

promise me
you'll take my fugitive memories,
promise
you'll smash them for me.

GOING UNDER

Keep me alive with blood transfusions
from heaven
filled with harmony and honest words.
At the surface

I emerge from the exhausted sea
alive with Aphrodite wisdom,
a quarrel between our mythologies
as Greek Gods,
now bask in my altercation.

In this dispute
between invisible and ancient worlds,
in drastic circumstances
under floods
vodka, love and Metaxa — wasted slow time

when death started to agree with me,
when death giggled
then became a refuge,
a shot of alcohol for my sanity.

LOVE LETTERS

I always thought that time does tell
But it keeps silent.
Give my clothes, all of my notes,
Give them to the less fortunate.

Patent shoes
Electric blue, open-toe, six-inch heels
Old worn unfashionable shoes.
Put them inside a box,
Light green, Earth printed box with a lid.
Give them to the less fortunate.

I left every lover of mine
Handwritten, toxic-scented
Malnourished and immature words,
Modern love letters.

Check my top drawer—
Under the tiny pink journal
That has a bouquet
Of flowers on its hard cover.

Everything you have ever written or worn
Shines brighter when you are dead.

Vow to me you will mail them out,
Walk to the post office
Make sure you have the correct postage
Let them fly across the dead blue sky.
Let them know

They are from me,
That I forgot to sign my name.

MARY JANES

I sat beside you in red shoes.
We watched the hockey game,
The Habs won.
We were sea engulfed
In the aftermath of the party.

We made love like lovers do
Every part of me, you knew
As though it belonged to you.
You know it didn't.

Oui, je me souviens de tout.

We recited poetry
On Rene-Levesque Street,
When the papers were fat
And humid on display
Each pointless line by line—
Marking our deep scars,
They are dying to live.

We should bury them, I say.
You know, You and I
Beneath a tombstone   .
Marked,
Poets die here
With no date of birth or death.

Oui, je t'adore.

I screamed, stop the car!
I never drive down this fucking street!
I don't know where it goes,
I need to visit London.

I quoted Prince: *You're on your own.*

Secrets have a way
Of becoming company,
And what would Sartre say?
Peering through your peephole
Everyone knocking
At your door?

Ma vie n'a jamais était dans un bocal.

Time has always been a liar.
I thought, this is what love feels like—
I think you made me sick
I think you made me your trick.

There is someone new for you,
Other lovelies
With shiny Mary Jane shoes and
Inky blue purses. Their wallets fat and mint green—
They match your ego.

L'amour est toxique, l'amour est Metaxa

I stumble
Past the poetry bookstore,
All the pretty pictures, how they glitter
From beyond the glass
Framed and lovely—

My name will never be there,
How death resembles a brick
Or how the sky bleaches labels.
I have become another dead poem
Glued to a broken liquor bottle,
How death stalks
From below the cracking glass.

CANCER

I locked myself away in my notebook
for perseverance
they gave me seven months to live then die.
My little Moulin Rouge, I died with you
from cancer,
I was reborn
a virgin girl at thirty-nine.

I can read emojis like poetry,
take photos under the moon
in foreign countries
full and glowing in sherbets,
watch my father take his last breaths —
I love you Daddy.

I fed him morphine
tabulated his death on sign-in sheets,
made his bed approachable,
candles and big bouquets. Greek delicacies
birthday cake.
I let in the strange neighbors who I hated —
They watched like China dolls,
a live reality show.

Oh, what cancer does to spirited bodies,
what it did to his merrymaking eyes
unforgettable and shaking,

I will remember him.
I'll be thirty-nine forever
he'll be sixty-eight forever. He'll be
my dead father forever now.

They always say,
it's just hereditary
it's perseverance
how Death follows the living around.

PERSONIFY ME

The trees speak in Shakespearean sonnets,
The tulips write short memoirs
The honeysuckles smell of metaphors and similes,
Vines are connecting complex sentences.

The sun has exotic eyes—
The moon tells of faraway lands
The ocean never leaves you…
Grass has flushed secrets.

The gardenia makes you altruistic,
The plants surround you with conversation
The sky watches over your insecurities,
Mountains sense your fears then embrace you.

This earth keeps you stirring coffee.
The seeds have this hope you only see in newborns
Branches love how all the seasons
treat them with respect,
Waves let you be yourself.

The rivers turn to dictionaries—
The deserts unfold unwritten novels.
You are this somber, mirthful universe
Another particle rising in a gust,

A bursting spirit in a lament of bones.

THE WITCHING HOUR

It never happens quite as planned,
the dead have unsaved destinies.
Death keeps surprising me
waking me

at three-in-the-morning
when the undone is possessed,
a sobbing call from Greece—
despair
sinking
our melancholic knees
bend to the downtrodden carpet.

Glioblastoma
cancer,
our hearts ache
with this longing to see
everyone who abandoned the homeland.

We know all the brain tumor definitions,
Death's sword keeps poking at me—
inevitable how it rips you apart
with a neck snap, an accident,
our house doctor calling
the shadow's stranger in my head.

LIE

People keep lies in their pockets
like bubble gum packs,
rhinestone wallets
dangling car keys
nestled baby pictures,
those wallets with hidden photo slides.

I tell a fib and my heart pounds
my nose grows —
like a female Pinocchio,
I need to be spanked
to rectify all my childish lies
like a real girl.

DECADES OF ART

I can lie like a jazz singer
on a sultry bed
in a torrid nightclub.
It's the 20s sliding inside humid
Chicago bars

I am a little girl, wonderfully sacred
and scared of consequences.

Nothing can be wrapped up as perfectly
as pink bodies, naked in the daylight
wet and sweltering on wrinkled sheets,
whispering red sweet secrets, like candy
on sky blue Sunday mornings.

I lie on the grass after a music festival
free from law, handcuffs
rules. It's the 70s
and we made it
out alive. We saw Jim, Jimmy,
Janet at the hotel. Patti was doing
a poetry reading in NYC.
We were the best observers and
the weakest artists,

no year and nothing to do
but straddle the centuries.

TUMBLE

Statuesque as a supermodel
or as buff as a bearded hipster,
everything you love
hard
dearly
can and will break,
tumble—

like ice into glass
or like ornaments knocked off plastic firs,
like empires
Amazon trees
a bra before sex

bitter bedroom
blackout blind,
a dead front lawn
with no green gardens.
Mediterranean sheets
with old and idolized secrets—

Dreams never whispered
or devoured,
complete loneliness bearing
no comedic breaks,

brimmed glass with cracks,
frigid and hard-mouthed
I am depleted,
abandoned by the half-truth
of all this clockwork.

PRESERVATION

It's a *thing* now
these days
every day
one day
today
tomorrow
every hour
to be a hashtag: a post-modern
bookmark for a self-published
book of poetry.

But love goes to die like that,
I've been guilty of that.
That *thing*
to make my future history
from my grandfather's epic
bedtime stories. It's no wonder
I have this dark imagination.

Film slides monstrosities of World War II,
bloody mounds of eyes in black and white
trenches of pneumonia,
Greek war stories my grandfather recounted
sad paper eulogies.
Eight sleeping in one room,
village life
outdoors a dirty bathroom,

lentils and bread for meals
stealing cucumbers
when electricity was a dream
before TV had color,
when lanterns were necessary.
Ancient stones
death as survival.
Preservation of your symbolism,
who you are makes you what you write.

But real love bleeds in inks
with an old fountain pen—
reality twists the mind's honeysuckle,
it has epically arrived!
An organic direction
a dark web leading somewhere penniless,
finally content
inside the mouth of limbo
where humility becomes the *thing.*

NO VACANCY

I slept under crumbled bridges,
car lights reflecting pothole prisms,
when I lost my soul to the gods of:
drugs
wars
alcohol
dead poets
sharp philosophers
listless writers.

Our glowing graffiti—illegal,
Polaroids, opioids
a tower of glossy tabloids—
past inflated—dated bottles
majestic little lanterns
erupting enlightened

you filled in a spotlight for me.
In neon bars I slaved in,
smoky
local
emptied, lonely rebel—
another female poet fitted slave,
I became your Metaxa maid.

No more niceties.
As the antihero you were made to be:

under a highway bridge
ashamed
stuffed inside a glass pillow evoking
cult leaders.

A revelation I named Vacant Lot.

CAPE COD

If you cannot find their addresses
Roll them inside Metaxa bottles.
Drive to the brim of the ocean,
Cape Cod when rising water
Feels as freezing as an icy
Tundra. Wrap them up in
Pretty silk bows of blue.
Find recycled seashells,
The ones never meant
For any storybooks
Filled with poetry,
That only ghosts
In our separate
Underworlds
Can marvel,
Then read
Aloud.

INSOMNIA

I can't sleep the way I used to,
or love again
or be the same. I know
the layers of books swarming my bed
ready to devour nightmares.
It took no time to think this—
write to you— this.
I wait for you to like it
I want you to have it,
this time
I want it bookmarked in your head.

I am such a nuisance
smelling my old thesaurus,
guarding its tattered pages
as the internet can not do—
the past meaning more than the future,
I wonder if I'll ever give these thoughts to you,
or manufacture the feeling instead.
It would be so terrible to go to the grave with it!
To waste it
and not regift it. This

is how killing myself feels,
never resting my cracked hands
my ripped thesaurus
staring at my bookends for suggestions—

holding my book close
just to fall asleep,
wanting none of it
wanting to be someone
who can sleep without writing you.

CRACKED HANDS

The words are peeking in at the oddest times
When proper daytime meets
Sexy hardcore night.
It wants to say so much,
But my icy heart dries up
Protecting from fallen ghosts.

But they do this last dance together
Before landing contently
On the frightening sheet,
I need to protect their vulnerability

Their need for me insatiable
From my thumbs to my purposeful voice,
They rely on me as a child.
Odd timings
Superstitions
Speaking their own language.

I want to make it stop
Between these moments
I want to scream *Go!*
Can't you see? I'm trying to forget!
These unwritten poems refuse to dissipate.

Once I hold them they're mine forever.
This woman's liberation

My aging hands in poetry books,
The moist earth under my bed
You—always hiding in my nightstand.
I made my words yours.
They suffer insomnia
Take fantasies prisoner,
Like a warped violin seducing its conductor.
Or the open-mouthed creatures
That are ready to eat me.

Sleep between the drunken days—
Metaxa then coffee,
New mornings.

My hands are tired
Of all this sunrise writing
Day-thinking
Pen marks
Unannounced visits from friends.
All these different cells in my head
Holding me hostage.

FASTING

When you had my wrists pinned
Like the ancient kings did
I never called you a farce.
When you made my heart pound
At a phone call
I heard how Earth shouts *doubt*

It is not a lie!
You can see through captured darkness
When the outdoor light disappears
For days and days and nights
You dream me up inside your mind,
It all becomes part of the recipe.
I wake up hungry for petty love,
Sitting on a street corner
My hands extended for crumbs,
But your love was fasting.

Sleeping made me whole
Loving you made me whole
Sleeping with you made me weak,
You filled my fridge
With hostility.

Like the untold story of Athena
On the same fucking page—
In-between our lives

Moments,
Bread slices.
Tangerine peels
Avocado eggs
Yogurt, honey, walnuts.
Your arms left no imprints,
You never offered me dessert.

I am a hand-baked piece of cake
With an abundance of tropic flavors.
You must have seen
My burnt edges,
The improper rise
Of all my sweet excuses.

ON BEING STARSTRUCK

So you want to be a poet,
you think you can
punch in and out?

So, you want to be famous?
Wear Gucci and parade
gleefully
across the American catwalks
with a book of your poetry in one young hand
and a list of writers
you'll never read
in the other?

So you want to be beautiful.
Smile with bleached teeth,
phone home and brag
make cash great again,
make words great again
keep the daily yawning going
boring again

entitlements
fake news
numbers
numbers
numbers
except you make it fresh and hip,

sitting in your chair all day
unstoppable:
your machine.

Wipe stars from your gorgeous dark eyes,
carry your own hurt
how bad you make the rest of us feel
artificial and digital.
Keep your day job at the bank,
being a poet is not good for the ego,
or the bank.
You'll grow mad like me,
you'll become a punch card.

ON STARDOM

Praised to be a star
praised to be epic
but at blank paper,
you sit and you glare,
you stare at it—in awe of what paper
can turn into

you buy your tickets with an allowance.
Take an airplane, fly to Washington
parade against sexual abuse
violence,
stand up for women's rights
and wave a flag,
taking selfies
with unlimited data

only you never rode a real plane
you never had a mother or father
experience horror.
You were never childless or aborted.
Never with another woman,
you never thought about it.

Your mother might be a suburban mother,
an all-around proper lady
who never justly
cracked open your soul. No one will know.

Hush now, but how can you?
There's stardom beyond these cribs, mobiles.
Are you turning into the ones you mocked?

Are you turning into another version of yourself?
You knew it all along
that eventually
you would become what you feared.

CONTRACTS

He is on his prosperous throne
Showing how he never loved me,
Only wanted city lights
On my naked flesh,
Only desired this glowing skin
Up against his armor,
Resplendent acts.

He made me see drinking
And driving was for savages,
Calm down, slow it down
Walk, don't run
But hotel rooms were for lovers.

Breathe, exhale, inhale
Don't be nervous.
Unaware of used books
That cross nations to tell
Stories that loved ones lived.

Promises are not made on top
Of twisted bodies, or over iced gin
Or in dirty one-night stand lobby bars.
Take the wine and my gift
Take my confession,
Throw it away. Be a gentleman,
Take it all away.

I never wanted to give it to you,
Promises are for churches!
Sunday Catholics
Praying advocates

On knees bent on faux leather,
Chanting contracts in tongues
To be repented, then appealed
By jealousy and neglect.

WOMAN WITH NO NAME

I am not every woman
I am not an extraordinary one,
I am not a beauty queen
Of words, or a porn star
Of flesh and X-rated nonsense.

No royalty lives inside me.
I am not entitled or branded,
No Prada purses, Louboutin shoes.
Princesses are from a dead generation.
They are pink and gendered
Falsely.

With heirloom candle holders
Striding down the stairs into the dark basement,
With no phones
Followers
No post every hot hour
No username or passwords,
No identity crisis.

This poem belongs to the nomad woman,
The forgotten Roma who lives in all of us
Who asked me for a light,
On the church steps of Corinth
Her dark eyes
Familiar, her skin like mine
Beyond the realm of titles.

ROOM 681

I made up my own memoir
of how lovers like us lie dazzled on stained sheets,
naked, saturated and full
nude bodies staring at a 70s plaster ceiling—

How many lovers have been here before us?

I looked at your body, held our breath
and memorized your stare
chalked our silhouettes in my head,
ones I'll fill in later.

MAKING MY LISTS BEFORE DAWN

Even if it looks as if I am living my life

I am always writing in my head

about the time my hydrangeas stopped
blooming and turned green

that time I waited inside the Met looking at
the Greek statues and you never showed up

going to the top of Tokyo and almost barfing

your manicured hands on my pre-teen skin

the apartment number I lost my virginity in

picking you up after a meeting for a latte

crying in a bathroom with blood on my thighs

confessing to a tombstone

never going to church except for weddings
and funerals

loving you more than you ever will

expecting too much from nothing

making lists with dog bones, a tablecloth and
mouthwash

and still you somehow squirmed yourself
into my words again

without even trying.

DEFINITIONS

My love language
is all of you,
please leave me stranded with your love
on a dead-end street
today, nothing exists at all
but centuries and old roots crying under the dying trees.
I'm angry—our antique furniture, centuries of soul
passed from one relative
to another space.

Tell me how death
and love
are inside my eyes—one minute
then gone in a second,
what's the definition of me?

Christina Strigas is a poet.
I read it in her bio.
She loves pasta with marinara sauce.
Another desperate poet with an ego?
I've run out of time to show you how
definitions are not looking for daylight.

I need poetry more than ever
to record my last sanities
in a safe place,
my own definition of myself

keeps shifting,
lost in moments
in poetic Middle Earth
the celebrated banter of past entertainments.

Prepare to combat my internal wars,
another shot of Metaxa—
downward heavy hearts are rarely merry,
the glass whispering in high definition
I love you, but who are you, mirror?

MISS STRIGAS

Sober nights between our love and beings
there were still moments given to this night,
bottled pain sweeping me away—drinking
in dreams, we pretend there were never fights.
You offered me corked gifts bearing no names
but none will be given again to me,
in this drunken stretch of familiar shame
therein you will taste my goddess to be.
Your listener, to your god angry voice
loving my drunk Greek lips, wetted with lies.
But I sit silently drowning in sounds,
lovers always say so many goodbyes—
drink from my cup of love and mistress sighs,
call out my name one final fall then rise.

I WANT TO BE HER

My neighbor smokes on her balcony
her blond hair in her eyes,
I miss that feeling,
of sitting down

enjoying the moment,
all the half-sentences.

She feels she deserves
a pause from life,
we all do.
Why did I quit smoking?
I need so many pauses,
still frames and more replay
buttons.

He still presses in on me
from a distance, still sitting here
over-analyzing the poems.
This one's a thoughtful burlesque
about another woman,
her open eyes
the dark experience,
her innocence.
I wish I was her, I imagine—
we could meet,
she tried to off herself and

maybe she's like me.
After all, aren't we all alike?

We could lay down on a blanket,
have a picnic at the cemetery
read dead memoirs and invent love stories,
mine and hers.

I wave to her and smile as she puffs
her smoke. She waves back
preoccupied.
I miss that old attitude—
I'm smoking, now leave me alone.

MEASURED TEASPOONS

Who loves me anymore?
People like to rehash old said shit
from five years ago
you had punched the door,
there's still a wrecked hole reminding me.

Pin their poetry on your forehead,
Jinx, touch red
it's identical now.
Someone brings you red wine,
you smile
chatting about reading and writing
you try to tell a joke
but fail miserably,
look around the room like a stranger.
That's not what I meant at all.
Who loves me anymore?

They see me with fugitive themes
forgive me for always leaving,
I flinch at the sign of danger.
Writers like to
play games,
hunting and recording
adventurous, dangerous love.

I can never tell who wants me
damaged and wounded from giving away
my secrets for cash
or fantasies for free.
If they do,
my ego never knows.

I can never tell time anymore.
It keeps rambling on and on like a song on the radio
that I can't listen to anymore,
indifferent to the wrinkles on my skin.
It's not Friday today?
When was my birthday?

I may be losing my witching powers,
maturing into the skin of my mother and father.
Perhaps they never existed
maybe normality is flowing into my veins.
Why are you wearing nylons with sandals?

I have become what I feared:
old and out of date,
expired
I have walked into a party
in the wrong era's outfit,
and when you try to explain it
you keep repeating
because I wanted to.
Yet you know that no matter
how you express yourself,

what you really want to say is,
that's not what I meant at all.

THE LEGEND OF A WOMAN

The mothers seek asylum
daughters plagued by ghosts
sisters running away from love
to drugs, depths of misery
killing our kinetic energy.

Grandmothers keep our stories
in their graves
use your cursive writing style
indulge in their wounds,
ravish yourself with your native past.

I will never know if the truth
of our ancestors
is as real as their tombstones.
Or if being buried beside them
will ever make us closer.

THE AIR AROUND YOU

Who needs to know the latitude of heaven
when the city lights
shine down upon our winter skin?
Your kisses are full of lament.

I threw Shakespeare at you—
I tried to be romantic
by reciting his sonnets
but all you cared about was the
white shape of my ass in the air.

You had me the moment you saw me,
it was how you grabbed me
like I was yours before I knew it.
I love you, don't say it back
let your hands do the talking instead
how they'd melt into the air on my legs.

Years later you breathe skeleton dust—
dead love affairs,
trapped in the prison of your life,
circling it like a vexed wolf
I imagine
it kills you beautifully.

Some thoughts are better left
stuck inside your throat,

like a tiny piece of grey hair
coughed up,
then poured down into a poem.

THE WAITER

The waiter took care of me
like the lost lover I never had. He catered
to me, my every whirling vegan need.
No need to explain myself.

This young hip waiter, full of Millennial advice
full of advice and alluring delight,
no one could love me
like he could.

My ex-girlfriend was a vegetarian
My ex-girlfriend was my soulmate
I wondered why strangers told me these things,
then he asked me why I didn't like meat.

I ate beet salad without goat cheese.
Walnuts, raspberry dressing
steaming quinoa with wilted kale,
basil leaves, white wine,
we talked quick shit about love.

Why aren't you still together?
I needed to know why
he gave me a painful look,
put down the check,
She passed from cancer.

I slid out the cash. Fresh greens
and chocolate coins,
I gratefully gave him a good tip,
far beyond my means
She would have liked you, he said.

DAMNED

I can turn into a vampire for you,
lips on your neck
I want to walk over puddles with you,
write until four a.m.
when I'm sober and naked
in bed with you.

But I am busy in my head
over-thinking
Damn you
confusing grand love
damn your sunset nights,
damn all your days.

A role out of another movie plot
me, this willing damsel
you, the charming man.
I had the love of my life
for six nights
I was your damned woman.

READ ME SOME YEATS

The philosophy of men
who lust to tamper moments,
more than frail human emotions
reasoning about war,
or the paintings at the Sistine Chapel
comparing wits,
this injustice of love.
The constant remains of the
closed gates of poetry —
Anons

Closing in on you
you find your own book in the street trash,
you imagine a young girl throwing it out, mumbling
I don't get it.
Who can ask for more?
Proof of your own incompetence,
proof of effort.

Inside your night table is more proof.
On your bookshelves are even more
limitations
a love that struggles.
Read me some Yeats,
The Selected Poetry,
The 1974 edition,
The One.

The one that explains the meaning
of the gates—still nothing will be forgiven.
Tread softly
use your best reading voice
lull me to love with suffering words,
I'm only a woman.

BURIED

I saw the ocean come alive
A subtle body
Falling to the water in music notes.

Turquoise notes on sandy seas,
Burgundy rocks between my toes
Oily sunscreen on my olive skin
Black revealing bikini,
There we were in heat
Like animals in spring.

We knew what the ocean between us meant
I had thirty minutes to love and leave you,
And three minutes to hate you
To end this nonsense.
The sea had eyes of empathy
My empathy spilled into the blinding sea
You brought nothing but time,
Something we never had.

When you quietly hoisted yourself
Out of the hourglass sand
I buried you under it
Hid your tidal wave love,
Emerged a pillar of concrete
With a sculpted marble wreath

Wilting ocean roses, seaweed
Tongue-tied and bloody,

Letting me believe in mermaids
For a few hours
Then moving to another country,
A non-existent country
Of no origin,
For another cosmic time
To a land of another woman.

DAY DRINKING

I will never meet you again.
Move on to the next high heels
it's a new age of grey-haired beauty,
you have the pick of the old.

Look away from my curves
the wine bottle shape of my boy hips,
all that lassie talk, porn channels
it leads to nothing.

You exist in another year,
our time travels separately,
my collection of seasons clean up
words during spring.

Today a Zinfandel is appealing
sitting in the rose garden alone,
spread out nude on a blanket circa 1800s
is where you'll find me happily
day drinking.

SELFIE

Your lies are ruins,
eyes like sloppy mud holes
the midnight,
it sucked up your honesty
spit out whipped cream
down the screen melting

for flatter. Painted rouge—pinched lips,
cinched hips
squeezed in by your own moon's
lunatic ways.

Your double entendres
capture no one of my interest,
we see inside the lady-in-waiting,
the vicious nightingale
sucking up to men like a succubus.

Your lover
and all the other hard magic kings
come inside to save you,
from your marriage
from mundane sex,
kids
chores
laundry
gardening

and your tiresome midlife crisis;
apathetic loneliness,

its nastiness chained to our screens.
I hope your husband will see.
You and your dirty handcuffs
made from others' misery.

Keep your dolly parts hidden
from prying husbands
and narcissistic sloppy old men,
desperation is creeping in,
the monitor is curdling.

THE GALAXY OF YOU

I wanted to be balancing
Between your hemisphere
Vanish away on my wings—
Pursuing the culprit of dreams
But my bubble bath will make do.

It keeps me floating alive
Nothing can burn me
Home and staying alone,
Writing
About our unmade plans
Unmade bed
Stories
All the depleting funds—
Act sane.

Bookend past.
I am too much
For anyone,
Offer me nothing
But the moon and atonement.

STRANGER AT PARTIES

I will not be expecting
anything. I left my empty drink on the table.
Vodka. On the rocks ice and truth
discreetly glancing around the room like a bachelorette,
disgruntled face
hunchbacks with lusty eyes
partaking in indolent small talk,
disillusioned and dumbfounded
I left the party to live
alone and pathetically reckless
in my own indifferent heart.

I abandoned the stranger
in a dark crowd where the music played
in murmurs and low beats,
time warp of hits
for averted people like this.

He wanted all the things
I could never give, love that swoons over deeds
love that eats cake for breakfast
love that kisses hypercriticism.
A love that creates a natural phenomenon,
a scientifically perfect woman
ready to mingle at a party in a heartbeat,
smile on cue

depart on command,
a stranger hovering
transcending
to an alley behind the muggy back corner,
the stranger saying
It's not your time yet.
We are all the creatures we love to hate.

I can never give anyone else more
objects, jewels — greed.
I hate being at parties this way,
making mental nametags,
drinking and smoking cloves until the
heartsick saloon door
swings back,
more people I love to hate.
I'm out of favor

more lines to write
more fat to combat
ailments
doctor appointments to make.
I am waiting
for all my undesirous traumas
only to be left reluctantly disappointed,
the future
this inevitable tombstone
beginning at 1968

it will end on a year I'll never know,
still disappointed
for expecting a full glass.

PLUNGE

Healing bodies made of cold sweat
flat sheets of four-hundred percent Egyptian cotton
connects the shame

in death trap puddles
they think they only have
one body to love.

It's a sex urging trap
a fake idealistic fall into a ditch
of cheap motels and pimped out cars.

They are holding onto moments
not prose,
she clasps like a lost & found key
that once belonged to her diary.

This is what desire looks like in a silent motel.
Surrounding him, a locked fence
on a bed blessing a naked body.
Want nothing more,
there is no key for this.

No questions and do not respond to his
perfect lies. He has somewhere to be,
you have nowhere to go.
Furious nights

together you had,
the room was witness
hours of wordless sex,
hard-pressed touching
urgency, hasty parting
cumming

he fishes out his keys
then makes a sexy exit.

NEW YORK MOMENTS

Write a poem about New York moments.

Unacquainted bookworms on Saks Avenue
We were searching for a used bookstore,
Affected by your needy love
I can show you the best time of your life.

You were so confident, I let you walk ahead
This is where Hemingway stayed
Here is the best coffee shop in Soho
Up there on that rooftop, best view of the city
Hand in hand in front of museums, skeleton art.

Christmas gifts in April
Displayed in the windows,
We happily passed
Jaguar biographies
Old record shops
Let's go in here!
A-Z of past hits

Next stop
A pair of Christmas tree earrings
A Rumi book for lovers,
This place never dies
It continues where we left off:
Look ahead, forget the past

I'll never be the same person.
You forget everything
I remember.

DROWNING IN CARNATIONS

I could never be true to myself,
I apologize for the past
present and this dusty gamble dead future.
The benefit of this damp
need to be loved,
to be swallowed up whole by your mouth.
I apologize for honest cruelty,
for changing into this
when you could not.

You were not who I thought you were,
I was not who you wanted me to be.
We abandoned our fixed purpose,
when marriage happens
we cease to see this.

Bitterness is not sweetening this,
it is prevailing— this aging
is ice-skating over my dreams.
My dried carnations are freezing
and you wanted lively and in love.
Watch them die as I think of you.

Drowning in velvet carnations,
how bad would it have been?
To hold each other down and kiss in public?

My dear husband
to run far away from this pool of life?

The dried-up smell is awakening
under wrinkled ambitious poems,
our decade old sheets
that got me thinking
and you're just blatantly naked and asking,
Do you want the lights on or off?

HER SIDE

There are two arrows
pointing toward spotted hearts,
one restless and one mournful

damned one for her lover
of the cracked truant night
the one who escaped his hanging,

who loved her blinding outbursts
cried over her at first,
laughed at her wit and charm

another arrow to aim for the one
who stayed put, her faithful man,
towards the other part of her descent

a man growing deeply out of her mouth
falling for her poetic side
down her pretty lips,

she has listless meaningless qualities
filling her wide mind,
exaggerated power

a taste that is dawdling
she cannot choose between
destiny and reality

her glory, pointed poisoned tips
she is the fugitive of nonsense,
arrow landing far from field,

she is the only witness
to her own rage.

LACUSTRINE

It is dry in my soul,
all the ancient lakes have an abundance of stories
eroded into vanishing valleys in me

no man ever traveled in
this length before hidden lacustrine deposits.
No man but him
the woodman,

with robust strength
height, size, body, eyes.
Built up histories of affairs
an inferno of tornado pasts

his name does not matter now,
he owns too many—
Don't ask too many questions,
it's not your business
how, when, where, why.

He had her in his forest
along discarded trees of women
apathetic with unknown titles
he said, *this is not how the story ends,*
you can and you will

but she couldn't and she can't.
We could lie on my bed and write—
something about each other,
pretend we are poets from another era,
you and me.

He said so many things she will never repeat
only in her head these lines live,
not even in a poem.

TRAVELED TO THE HIGHLANDS

Met herself in the center of a lake
where the singing waters wrapped their calmness
around her
where the green landscape comforted her,
she never made it

her desire to end it was more than her desire to start,
their paths skinned her knees

she threw tiny rocks
of stories in the lake
that reminded her
of a past life that they dreamed together,

we were married once and had two children,
we had matching tattoos on our arms

she'll add it to her tiresome fire,
in Canada
where it burns silent by Lake Superior
she is silent now,
Sleeping Beauty with no fairytale prince.

CELLAR LIES

Once my own madness
mixed into the mahogany of yours
I feared my vulnerability,
discovered how your boredom loved me,
sensed your cellar lies

in my cold Greek veins
on your tipsy lips.
But God doesn't like drunks
hiding in cellars

like we're the devil's joke
shackled by Glutton's fault,
voluptuous dark
Alan Watts and spiritual connections—

a willingness to love this sadness,
these witty faults of mine
beyond the cracks of the dark cracked floor
plaster on aging walls.
You pour me a damaging glass,

a riddle of wine
where your perfect pour
unearths my desires,
you pour me my punishment.

BARBAROUS LOVE

I stumbled over my own books,
our unassuming past
and sculpted myself into
a flash memory

a half-siren, a naughty whore
sacrilegious,
a woman with no written rules
for you. You made me up,
manipulated to be yours,
Spirit Artists.

You had my legs wrapped
around you like gift ribbon,
soft edge-of-Earth thighs
a thesaurus of erogenous zones,
deep minded touches
foreign thoughts,
overworked mind.

You threw all my clothes,
my modest bra on the dresser
my bright socks in-between the sheets.
We're going to hell.
Why is this familiar motel named Hell?

129

If you take my body
don't give it back.
If you speak my name
forget it.
If you tell another soul
I'll never forgive you.

Please leave me my damned soul.
It needs to rest like a young girl's,
not an old married woman.
I am going to hell with or without you.

One day we will meet at an empty reception hall
in front of elevators on dirty floral carpets
that will seduce your ethics
up and then down
and onto your knees,

Hell is not as cold as a hotel icebox,
it is the desire to love someone
you're not allowed to.

UNBALANCED

Social media is taking over brains,
start writing on paper again
buy new flashy pens to inspire
start thinking for yourself

find soul
they want to control our intake
outtake, monitor our every subtle move,
this institution does not believe in arts & lettres,
the government gaslights us
breaks our words up into hashtags,
promotes capitalism
power, dishonesty.

Thunderstorms ache
trees have branches of philosophy
flowers contemplate your religion,
bring the forest to the podium,
stop scaring sanity.
The world is cracking up;
television testing you
government disclaiming you,
social media warps our overstimulated minds,

the poet's unbalanced addiction.
My brain needs zen, not more
and more applications,

data
more stimulation as to who follows
this rejected poet,
this artist.

A few times in my life, I had great connections,
but life takes breaks.

In 1991
we talked more, called each other
at the university
with other academics
as young as twenty
professors opened their homes—
offered us white wine and on Mexican night
we ate enchiladas, black beans.
I met Prof V's eleven-year-old son,
talked grad studies.
Victorian poets
thesis advice,
a night of talking about writing,
all forgotten sentences now
nothing recorded, posted,
monitored.

All the poets are out now
competing for internet approval,
I'm still at it in my own way.

Where are they now?

It's funny how
that professor used my words
how he had been grabbing at my coat,
my twenty-year-old self
looking to his young son
as an exit.

All we have now is isolation
and our rejection,
it's just more apparent.

CHRISTMAS EVE

keep your arms open,
it's Christmas Eve
and who can fix who?
it's beautiful to me
remembering you,
maybe you recall the beat
and still feel the jingle
of my childish knocking.
you opened the door,
wooden, carved, aching
to be touched as if
I was the only gift
in your holly arms.

WRONG SORT OF RIGHT

Is this marriage?

Tied inflicted loneliness
to dreams, unromantic
your arms, far too large
your charm
your grasp, when under water
wet and relentless,

half-way alive, married to marriage

thrust me onto a highway —
smacked my face in reverse,
man-made
between melting white lines

paralleling half-dead

my laughing letting go of body
with flattened eyes and a treacherous mouth,
robotic talk.
I spoke about dying,
in ways you never loved

tongues wagging the living.
I can't take back anything,

marriage walks us into graves unannounced.
Carry me past the threshold,

kiss my wrong sorts of right
all of my sarcastic good humor you adore,
mauled under my tired backyard
smashed flower pots and buried door knobs.

Love me like a bridge protects its water,
I'm floating under you,

Yes, this is marriage.

A MOMENT IN THE LIFE

Dammit Chrissy, you're always writing
I rolled my eyes like an impetuous child
at an authoritative parent,
I tweeted
Just when you think you know someone, they change.

He annoyed me this morning.
Always looking in the mirror asking
How do I look?
I was on my laptop
not looking at him,
You did something to me. What did you do?!

Nothing. I continued tweeting
Being brave can make you uncomfortable,
but it's necessary.

I can't say where these thoughts derive,
there is a solid reason for words,
How are you being brave?
All these strangers in another space,
internet friends.
I have all of these poetic discussions /conversations
with all these real people
inside my phone.

Chrissy, I have to go to work
Does it match?
Put your phone down.
But I can't, I'm writing now—
back to the laptop,
save my manuscript, charge my phone
and then I walk him to the door,

tell him *I love you.*

THE RENDEZVOUS

Poets need each other, they feel so lonely
they could die from it.
They need a muse more than a human.

She knew his hasty eyes,
she read about them in a past life,
the one that she imagined at the bookstore
while waiting impatiently
in an aisle he never showed up at.

She thought she saw him at the edge of last century,
between the dead seasons
between bookshelves,
but it wasn't him
in a photo, under the fog of his eyes—
she saw a future.
She told him on the phone,
I hold onto my demons for good luck.

But we poets are delusional,
making up stories, scenes, bookstores,
libraries, places, settings.
Confusing them into one tale
for the greater good of the poem.

She sat upstairs in the children's section
reading Robert Munsch books,

pretending not to look around or care
that he was absent,
or that she was childless. She thought
Stories don't always end just because we write an ending.

He had a Hollywood name,
a lie she found out years later.
A "catfish" it's called.
The shop had been full of people that day,
she smiled at a little girl.

In New York, everything always feels romantic,
even being stood up at a bookstore.

THE HUNT

She imagines where he is now,
New York walking down a crowded street
on his way to a meeting

Mexico City meeting
after meeting,
no time to take a dip

Venice, by a fancy restaurant
overlooking the city,
Vancouver, the view from his

hotel room spectacular. In Xiamen
eating noodles
with chopsticks feet up—

jeans on, bored, exhausted
in his upscale hotel
alone for hours

he feels abandoned,
only calling when wanting something.
She imagines him laying on the bed.

Chasing her is a curse
he wants afternoon sex,
midnight phone calls

coffee dates, chocolate croissants,
two-bottle wine dinners,
mad sex in changing rooms,

she cannot give him any of it.
He wants her secrets
to always travel between them.

It makes no sense to be so lonely,
as the song plays
he imagines her sleeping

naked with someone else
he can't believe
how he let himself get caught like this.

A POET'S WAY

Poets mow the lawn with words
plaster homes with nouns,
smoke cigarettes with a sigh
wine with grief, loss, love,
always expect to be entertained,
amused.

Poets are the outcasts
the chosen ones
destined to write of the fears
no one dares to watch

smiling when they need
some money for coffee,
they turn blood-red
when you call them Poet.

High on imagery
explaining how Gods disappear,
how beauty stains us and
the true meaning of Truth,
how our different books smell.

CONVERSATIONS WITH THE DEAD

Never followed Dad's advice.
Wish I did now.
In '89 thought his words archaic,
in 2017 I'd say he was
pretty damn smart.

My daughter will roll her eyes,
one day remember ancient adages
maybe in 2050
she'll finally agree, nod her intelligent head
and remember this like me.
This is hindsight:

the unanswered phone,
Black Bell phone on the kitchen counter
ringing endlessly, going to voicemail,
no one checking again

I can hear his voice from the dead,
rough, yet gentle
faintly forgotten, I press play:
I thought you were home. I hate these damn machines.
His broken English sounded perfect.

This is the cycle,
my mental clementine peels
my form of existential awareness,

an endless study of the silenced voice
playing his recording to remember,

because tombstones can't talk back.

ZEIBEKIKO

Clap your hands
stand up now
place the Metaxa shots on the dance floor,
I am dancing a Zeibekiko
the way I was taught by my father,
it's our song

knees on the cracked floor
surrounded by chipped white plates
tight dress wrapping me up like jewels
mouth wrapped around the glass,
hands up
singing and shouting
Opa!

Let the language of poets
statuesque lyrics light you alive,
songs about pain, loss
metaphors, similes, alliterations
in bouzouki strings
tragic scenes,
epic crying love stories,
men wanting women
women chasing after trains
goodbyes, last year's love affairs

regrets, missed chances
all the while
the bouzouki plays,
even men cry if left discarded
alone, abandoned on the floor,
so I stay.
I see why Henry Miller
loved Greece so much.

Makes you want to speak Greek,
shout *Opa!* Now is the time to
pretend to be Greek
learn what heartache Notis Sfakianakis is,
singing *O Aetos,*
a bird flying, a metaphor for love
leaving. It dies free and strong
the night sky, how the heavens hug the bird
all singing along;
What hunger is picking at him,
picking at his psyche?

Round tables of red wine
oldies with joy in their hearts,
watching and clapping afar a dying generation
death glooms.
Tzatziki, feta cheese
taramosalata, spinach pies, cheese pies
lamb, lemon potatoes
Greek salad: tomatoes, onions
cucumber, olive oil, oregano.

Bottle of red, bottles of white
singing to the lyrics
hearing their stories,
Was she running after a train?
Was his body and soul aching from neglect?
What were the last words his lover said?
Gather around now

clap your hands around me
down on your knees,
bouzouki strings
now match the steps
one, two, twirl
bend to the floor
another shot,
knees to the ground
Coward! I'm putting on a show!
You know the lyrics now.

More shots
hot grateful liquor drops
looks like honey, tastes like bitter love—
it's only three a.m.
and there are still heavy songs
left to dance to.

We'll be the last to leave
dancing in this joy
until the light dims away,
and the darkness explains it all.

HOW TO HIDE THE TRUTH

She chews peppermint gum— *Pop!*
She spits it out when she sips her whiskey
hating the taste
done with it,
he chews it

all night,
hides it below his wicked tongue,
when they fuck
it's still there.

He took her to his apartment,
banged her up against his bed
and twice
she came.

He chews gum while fucking
how awful it must taste to him,
kissing her
he cannot taste what's under
the tangling Greek currants
the tangy breath on her lips,
the raw taste of her mouth

that should not taste like dry peppermint,
she spits out her gum—

she spits him out,
preferring the taste
of a dirty mouth.

CURSED LIES

Plant your blooming lies,
I have a shovel in my garage.

Let them sprout—
whether loving or drinking you is worse

you are still on the menu.
No one grows these fantastical visions

better than my human hands and mind,
or the furious devil,

what will you think of my dreams
when they stop believing in themselves?

On the midnight patio
overlooking the backyard,

drunk in the rocking chair
the shadows are love bombs.

I tilt on this axis,
I dig out all your truth.

MYTHOMANIA

It feels like every time you leave the crowd worships
your entrance
a rising crippling ache I can see you are a slave to it,
compounds fawning over art
into a state of constant wanting fanatical cheers
waiting to be loved wanting to be bounced
waiting to be ignored wanting to be celebrated
waiting to be cerebrally embraced emerging stronger
by someone who can only exist when both of us
combine
in my own head, a sneaking myth a grandiose
desperado
swaggering with pretentious tales full of myths and
secrets,
maybe I'm the crazy one, maybe I'm the realist
or maybe it's us both
or maybe you are.

METAXALONE

I am living in the fog of an old world
around downtown on Hooligan Avenue
on our astral plane
we are unsubstantial now,
lost addresses where we once met
there you are, I murmur to myself,
it's him I bet.

Do I inject you with the love of my sky?
Instead of the pharma sedative of your kiss?
Breaking bones,
I'm aging every day
with your noose around my neck.

Do not open my dark drawer
there's a drug war in there,
in my prison head
you'd feel wonderfully
inactively dead.

I am grey-footed
prowling in middle of day,
stumbling on the concrete
no gravity under or around me,
Helios left me to the dark—
there you are, I convince myself,
it's him I bet.

POETS ARE WRITERS FROM HELL

People think it's easy to
sit
sit
all day
and write
bang on an unpretentious typewriter with fervor,
glitter with words.
kick humility out the window,
what do they know of work?
mowing and scratching
hungry
sifting the garden for new
seeds of imagery,
not make money
till
dig for words
then wait,
wait forever for your rejection letters.

maybe they're laughing,
collecting your submissions
as proof of who you're not.
years of this.

no partner wants this,
this shame
this kind of demure limbo,

this majestic love.
treasure any letters,
love them
frame them,
you
might one day publish them
in a noble newspaper.
glue them to your mirror
or hang them above your bed.

later
later down the line
when your fingers ache from typing,
your mind succumbing to rejection
you'll finally stop pretending,
and maybe
just maybe
you'll realize
you are a poet

and poets aren't best-sellers
we are the antiheroes,
so you want to be a poet in hell do you?

poets can be found everywhere,
in a modern kitchen
pounding meat
in a bathroom crying
on a toilet vomiting
in a boardroom meeting

in the backyard chatting
in a bathtub masturbating
on a bed napping
at the kitchen table
typing
typing
for hours

people think it's easy to
write
write
and as easy or speedy
as you do these things,
it's still a mystery
how these words
these infinite words
travel through our veins,
from the mind
to the fingertips
in seconds

cooking
the forgotten meal
on the stove,
phone ringing
buzzing
isolated
you land face-first
onto the honest front
of white paper,

you make your hell
a tiny bed of heaven.

THE APOLOGIES

Three a.m. searching for the earth she was born in
in snow that never melts
the final chapter begins again
                              I'm sorry I didn't clean the house.
The fucked-up way he said her name
as if it belonged to his heritage.
It got to her.

Every day changes her—
every new love kills her,
she never wanted to answer his message.
                                        Yes, he insisted.

Once with thirty years of need
riding over a city bridge,
she fell in love for the first time.
                                        I loved you.
Once, after thirty years of apologies
she fell in love for the last time,
                                        I loved you.
St-Laurent river unchanging
under her lovers,
death could crash inside her
unquiet
troubled,
full of cancer.

158

The dance of nail-biting sex
in two separate beds

I'm sorry I lied.

You'd think she made a thousand mistakes a day,
that grazing her Achilles heel
meant her funeral was approaching,
her lonely coffin of unedited manuscripts,

I'm sorry. I loved you too.

AMUSE ME

As he entered my mouth
I drenched in his need

his wit and humor,
groan across my nipples

evoking heat
a warmth of childhood.

darkness long forgotten,
rise another realm

my lips to let him sit.
enter my pores gradually

detach from the dirt.
my desperation is in the room

dirty wordplay
inching down my inviting throat,

touching my unbeautiful belly,
grotesque thighs

letting him get his money
off my old skin, rent is due.

LANDSCAPES

We posed for an old-fashioned camera
lost our negatives,
they're floating around in
attics now. The ancient city
labyrinth of surprise.
Our youthful eyes full of ideals.

We grabbed a cab
as if we could even afford it
pretending to have cash in our wallets
intending to run bloody fast,
teenage punks listening to Zeppelin
unlit cigarettes silhouetted between our fingers,
acting tough, puffs
times when being an artist mattered.

The mountain filled with faces
biking, races, calm walking
calm talking
an abundance of tourists surrounding,
we were dots on the globe
where Montreal starts to shine
its stars on us

snap a shot, turn on the flash
hive of voices
big city selfies,

empty plastic water bottles
tourists still snapping
taking shots of the Big-O—
You have guts leaving it all behind.

That's how I like my romances,
offensive as an insult,
our vulnerable smiles caught in moonlight
reading and progressing
down into a poem.

I like leaving it all behind, except you,
I can never leave you behind.

TYPEWRITER PAPER

Your hazardous reflection
has a history
of cracking souls on typewriter paper
they evolve into other characters,
find yourself here

with clacking thoughts of you
drumming letters,
pounding keys,
I think of how

stale crumbs of you
I wanted
I needed
absolutely none of you,
how many times can a woman say no?

If you aspire to love me
why run when I tell you to?
You're in your BMW speeding down the 40,
when did you stop dreaming of us?

Do not wait too long,
do not read more into this,
it's only art
it's not real

when these words pass
all that will remain
are these broken sentences,
created for your eyes
in this bitter typewritten poem
that you requested.

AN X AND AN O

Meet me at the lounge bar
I'm on your right
by the hotel lobby's brown leather couch when you come inside

she was already on the sixth floor
searching for his room number,
grey carpet, a hallway of silver numbers
heart pounding,
hitting the digits of his area code

she was ready for him months ago.
Drinking gin and tonic,
waiting for it
relaxed,
focused, under the bar table
he rubbed her
admiring her foxy jeans,

she had iced vodka with lime,
cold mouth, hot body
deathly nerves
small talk led to bigger,
anticipation of sheets and skin
sleek elevators led to bed.

Doing it to death
his mouth hot as the teenage sun

on glowing young skin,
and here they were again
removing their clothes
shirt, pants, socks
bra, underwear,
giggles and sex,
she was his wanting gift.

His playlist jumped boundaries,
they compared stars
traveling stories of exotic Turkish lands,
cities they passed through and
the vitamins they took.

The money they never had
travels they never went on,
family trees

voyaging to hell and heaven together,
writers
fingers and love,
how mortals coexist
with x's and o's.

RUMI LOVERS

He can move in and out of her
as Rumi lovers do,
the type of lover
who knows your body
before he touches,

the sort that knows everything
by asking.
The one to please,
send you off with prayers
give you god pleasure, madly
make sex turn to love.

Turn society to a foreign entity
in the sky of rich Canadian light
on a plane, behind the dreamy clouds,

an absurd projection from a dream.
You can touch ceilings, foreign skies
heights of such magnitude
that mountains become envious.

He makes the feeling of time slide
unforgettable ungodly hours
the body is spiritual,
over-loved and not hated,

between brilliant fantasy and bird-chirping reality
the opening of her soul

one with one another,
for hours of sexy darkness
hours of flesh
two spirits in one body
made to flow in love's unity
as a perfect shape, one
that they knew

as Rumi lovers know,
how to navigate
each other's thoughts, soul
pink skin, their bodies, one poem on a page.

OH, CANADA

Watching the sun rise is one of the most trusted
things.
I'm old school. Old soul for shining love.
In Greece, the sunrise overlooked the ocean,
in Canada, the sunrise overlooked Park Ex.

When I was eight
I saw Greece in your eyes.
I understood what the word "immigrant" implied.
All the looks, questions
Where were you born?
I'm Canadian. I'm Greek.
I'm Greek-Canadian.

I'm nowhere to be found.

I mostly feel like a sea animal—
life fish-hooked me
adored my Canadian skin, its delicacy,
flapping my fins in the air.
Olive complexion, dark hair and eyes.
Oh, you look Greek or Italian.
You have an accent.

Did you know the ocean grave is so silent?
There is no grandiose ocean here
Canada is civil, making no war.

Canada opens up its arms to immigrants like us.
It wets our words with ghosts,
not the ones in movies or reality TV,
the real ones that terrorize immigrant dreams.

Canada has clawed cold cuts on my skin,
the dry scathed skin of winter.
I'm allergic to the cold now
still translating documents for my mother since 1980.

They make me write about how she came to Canada
on April 29, 1960.
She had two birthdays,
my grandfather changed it to 1943
for survival
and now I'm filling out 10-page applications
to prove she is who she says she is
after living here for fifty-eight years.
It's always hopeless
when you can't speak the language
you live in—
but it is hopeful
to have a nomad soul.

You can be a stranger in two countries.
I see proof of that every day.

LAST CALL

She sat at the bar drunk,
insanely drunk, blurry with mixed
up feelings of love and sex.
she went to his top floor apartment
straight into his naked torso
spelling letters on his back,
motions in his name.
her delicate fingers
erasing years of misery,

is it tragic or poetic?

knocking her insides around
a glass bowl of fruit,
no longer drunk,
was it the alcohol? what was his name?
she could not remember
but this pain he has, she wanted to
make it go away

only fools love like this,
aimlessly wandering and not caring
if the other person is wearing a ring.
divorced three times,
cheated on his pregnant wife,
she grabbed her clothes to go,

left no number
no evidence that she was ever there

long after
the two-forty-five last call
his love,
a world where reality does not exist.
he made her see how it all begins
how it never ends
over and over,
take each other for granted.

CORINTH

Is it okay to be
rude for no reason?
The reason I love you is
not the right one

that comes to mind. I spread love of words
dressed in imaginary
half-ass wings, on a little Greek girl fragile
watch me breathe in and out Greek—
Crying in ancient Corinth

where centuries pass without trace
where my parents were born
in a small Greek village in the mountains
named Stimaga—
where my roots are

a city of survival and travel,
Jason settled there with Medea
where Pegasus became a symbol,
the myth of Arion,
how loving monuments is more graceful
than building walls of torment—
While awake – while asleep,
I am perfectly free of evilness.

The restless dream in sleep paralysis
falling wings deglorifying,
the past is buried now
where my father finished high school
where my mother finished elementary.

But even reason has a way of changing,
turning to outright wild lies;
this is where you were rude to me,
laughed at my home-made history lessons.

Go down to the village, wake up the family
or sleep-in,
then shout-out the morning for coffee—
I can't hear you now
I'm at the tip of my village
where I first met my grandmother *Yiayia Xristina,*

where these walls await
a new language you can never learn.

L&M

It's a gift to create you,
make my drink of choice
carry you around
under the armpits

in purses
to a café shop *Patisserie*
in the city *centre ville,*
feel the heat of your drink
down my throat
twisted carnival on the rocks.
Caramel colored love

color of its giving words,
I gave birth to this.
Struggling for years to be perfect,
it fucking made me run—
Gallop to an abundance of words
nouns, adjectives, verbs
then back to you, again
my bottle full
open-mouthed
pouring out
with all my minutes counted down,

tonguing Metaxa—
knowing its history

its label
of its five or seven stars, it kissed the years
off my Greek lips,
introduced me to my other self
my poet-self
my drunk tongue, my inebriation
and vile liberation,
typed it into this book,

you're holding me now.
Take good care of me please,
it took me years to get here.

APPOINTMENT

Talk to dead ghosts,
forget doctor appointments,
today is always Death.

Everyday reaps new novels
of reason, to hold our sun closer,
death anniversaries are the hardest to celebrate.
Wandering women like us
laugh and cry at the same start,

I am
writing your story, I am every man too.
I am every woman who contemplated death.
How to kill her husband
how to kill herself to survive.
Bring me my Doctor Death,
I will serve him my last poems
show him how I never really meant to die,
only on paper

I will tell tender-hearted women:
let go of stifled binary inhibition
let go of this image of men so distasteful
swish them in your mouth
then spit them out
cut them out into words,
instill your own thoughts.

I am right here for you
holding onto Doctor Life,
making my ghosts their coffee.

FIRST FUNERAL

I was sixteen, back from my New York City tour, my
cousins from Queens adopted me for three weeks and
took me to all the usual sites: Central Park, the Statue of
Liberty, museums and my favorite bookstores, walking
all over the city, in the back seat of an old Buick, smoking
pot, drinking liquor. No curfew for the teenage summer.

Your cousin John just returned from Greece
he is in the ICU
stage four
cancer
Hodgkin's disease.

Bits and pieces until I walked into his room—back then
in Montreal, his young skin too pale, room cold. All my
family on the verge of crying, holding back sorrow and
trying to be strong, my aunts holding icons, praying,
kissing his forehead, icon of Jesus, people crying and
screaming, fainting. We follow so many rules to create
a perfect death.

Black dresses, black shoes, black ties, black shirts, black
skirts, black pants, black soul. No makeup. No smiling.
No laughing while in line. Just nod and shake the
stranger's hand. It is how we show our pain, black
must surround us, darkness, the silence of the earth as
a coffin lowers.

Zoe se sas, over and over... You can't translate Greek expressions, or the way we think or drink Metaxa. Plastic empty shot glasses piled high in garbage cans. Heirloom goblets. ("Life to us" is the literal translation).

This is how life stops protecting you. *This is how we all end up* I told my sixteen-year-old self. This is how death can shut the blinds and never let you back in. This is how my first cousin dies at twenty-three. So I wrote him this.

Grief has us by the throat.

PATERA I

Your brown eyes changed us,
bony and sunken
fragile and lonely
on a bed when hours could have been months
so many last goodbyes—

we were never sure,
if time meant the same to you.
Death had its grip around your life,
seven months of this.

I drove to Sherbrooke Street,
scored comforting morphine
tracking the days,
gave it to you for release from your eyes
when your voice was gone forever.

Prepare the essentials for a funeral
death is tapping lightly.
Make your lists,
dig open the wet earth,
rely on human hands,
let the cold hands carry your years

in kindness, it fires back.
This isolated pain of the dead
inferno pyre,

an element of survival.
They stop breathing, you
stop feeling

a rapid devouring of time—
drink the shots.
Warm the dead body inside
kiss the forehead, wonder why
the dead won't need art again.

Watch strangers carry the body from the house
on a stretcher—
a red blanket tucked under his feet.

Patera means "Father" in Greek

PATERA II

I crashed on the floor
next to your dead body, Patera
You were wrapped in a red flannel blanket of fire.
Your last breath,
of three deep sighs . . . a matchstick
flaring-up a crowd of love,
we watched the horror.

Around your nailed feet
edges of years,
like a quick flame
your light disappeared,
brushed by fingertips
an odyssey of stops,
a heart-wrenching eulogy.

But the saints are calling you —
to dream on their bed of rose clouds,
they want your Good Friday bonfire.
Light up the glow father
Patera, kalinihta
goodnight.

When you died ten years ago,
the world shifted
Greece and its olives,
its braced trees

seem so distant now
miles of gravel,
a dead memory.

Epic to recall
how you stole cucumbers,
in your youth
raised on bread and lentils,
hand-prepared in a clay sink
in one room with five siblings,
how you got beat for days
walking miles to reach school.
No swings, amusement parks
or merry-go-rounds,
no lights on your village street,
only one telephone.

You left Greece with a five-dollar bill in your pocket,
a Greek-English dictionary in your backpack.

YIAYIA MARIA

She taught me how to love
raised us in a tiny apartment
while my parents worked,
five grandchildren in her arms.

My love of nature because of her plantings,
my first cup of Greek coffee
from her hands,
Stir, wait for the froth
lift the briki (pot)
ena, duo,
pour in a tiny cup
never forget the glass of water.

Her attitude snarky
mocking my choice of men
mocking my eccentric clothes,
sarcasm her music,
her spirit:
The afterlife will flow better now—
plan the rapid conception of midnight.

If you want your grandmother to pursue you,
after death
have a daughter,
bring air to her breath.

Hospital air is lovely when
you see your child for the first time—
Five-forty a.m., I created life
one push for twenty minutes,
no epidural, a natural birth.

Maria was born
reborn,
born again
her tiny head resting on my skin
like a kitten,
I lay there breastfeeding
breathing
caressing her baby skin,
smelling her
touching her dark full head of hair.

Now I lay all day
giving milk,
sleeping, eating, sleeping, producing milk
looking at the clock
missing the funeral.

You were supposed to be named Maria, after me,
there are already two Christina Strigases
in Greece. I had responded,
Don't worry Yiayia, when I have a daughter
I will name her Maria.

And Greg's parents
were named John and Maria,
and so are our children.
My promise at ten came true,
like the words I uttered after birth,
Maria, my dreaming daughter
I hope you have her spunk.

I gave birth, Yiayia died
two days apart, in life
ninety years apart in birth.
Your clothes didn't match!

Choking on food and asthma attacks,
not missing one wise-ass comment
she was always right,
but oh how she loved us
how she cooked lentils for us
how she stood up for us
how she laughed with us
how she cried when cousin John died,
how tough of a woman she was,
always standing up for herself
never backing down from men,
and that's what I liked best about her.

What I hated dearly,
her hemming of my dresses
her Prince outfits out of velvet curtains,
she never denied my creativity.

She taught me to be stronger than any man—
her attitude passed down to my daughter,
Maria.

I don't know how she did it,
but she did.

Yiayia means Grandmother in Greek

THE LAST POEM OF THE BOOK

Some lovers give you the world for three hours,
you go your own way
without an umbrella in a storm.

Some lovers love you for the right reasons,
yet you'll go searching
for all the wrong ones.

Some mothers spoon hate on a plate full of food—
your judgment
is forever misplaced.

Some fathers realize your worth instantly,
but you continue to love
the inevitable winters.

Some children wrap you with pride,
others follow their gravel paths
then come back as chameleons.

Some addictions are as lonely as a wolf,
where only strangers in the wind love you
hate you, for who you are not.

Some secrets you keep so silent
that crows can not decipher you,
it is only you and your clever mind.

ACKNOWLEDGEMENTS

Thank you, the reader, for purchasing this poetry book.

Thank you to all of my fans and followers who read me online. Thank you for your messages, your love, and your ongoing support.

Thank you to Alexandra Meehan for helping me edit this book so many times (I've lost count). Thank you for questioning every comma, break, semi-colon, period. Thank you for being my rock when my heart broke. Lex, you are my soul sister. Thank you for pushing my creativity to the max. I love you. This book could never have been without you.

Thank you to Metaxa for its ethereal magic—its power over all the Greek moments in my life.

Thank you to Syliva Plath and especially Anne Sexton, whose poems inspired me and changed my life forever.

Thank you to Greece, to my heritage, my ancestors. Thank you to the strong Greek women in my life. Thank you to my mom who stood up for me no matter what. Thank you to my dad who visits me and sings to me from the sky above. Thank you to the messages from the universe, to the divine feminine, to the divine masculine, to the light and to the dark.